Portraits of Aston and L.

2000

Photographs by Aston and Erdington
Photographic Society

First published in 2000 by
Brewin Books, Studley, Warwickshire B80 7LG

© Aston and Erdington Photographic Society 2000

All rights reserved

The photographers' moral right has been asserted.

Donations from the sale of this book will be
forwarded to the Stroke Association

British Library Cataloguing in Publication Data.
A catalogue record for this book is available from
The British Library

ISBN: 1 85858 182 6

Typeset in Meta and made and printed
In Great Britain by Warwick Printing Company Limited,
Theatre Street, Warwick, Warwickshire CV34 4DR

Aston and Erdington Photographic Society

A Brief History

The two predominant photographic societies of North Birmingham, have traditionally been the Erdington and the Aston clubs. Both have been in existence for around 100 years, and were formed and operated independently until their coming together in 1972.

As both clubs were regarded as 'important institutions', they have left us with the great legacy of club records, minutes and documentation of how they ran their affairs throughout their history.

The Erdington Photographic Society started its activities in 1892, and by 1903 boasted a membership of 31 fully paid up members including a 'Lacy W.Baldwin'. The tenure of the membership list tells us that at the turn of the century, photography was indeed the pastime of the local aristocracy and moneyed class. The working man would not have been able to find funds for an average camera costing 17 guineas, and membership of five shillings per person.

Much of the equipment, competition prizes and refreshments were donated by the club president, making this post an expensive postion.

On 11 December 1911, the club held its annual exhibition at Drayton Studios in the High Street, Erdington. In 1913, the society moved its headquarters to Church House in the High Street, and membership continued to flourish. Regular club trips are recorded to places such as Sutton Park, Kenilworth, The Wrekin and Stratford on Avon

Whilst the Aston club was established in the early 1900's, unfortunately its early records have not been saved. We know that Aston, Erdington and Handsworth clubs held a joint photographic exhibition in 1912.

Both clubs continued almost uninterrupted throughout the Great War, and we have a number of detailed accounts of lectures being given on subjects such as 'A Week in London Zoo' and ' How a Reflex Camera is Made'.

The first record we have of Mr A.E.Brookes (Arnold Brooks), later to become one of this country's most notable photographers, is an exhibition catalogue of 1929. The Birmingham Post of 11 March 1929 comments on his 'exceedingly high standard of work, including his Federation Medal winning print of The Docks Truro'. Arnold Brooks went on to be club president and the main driving force behind the Erdington club through to the time of its amalgamation with Aston in 1972. His work with the development of Bromoils is still legendary today.

The financial accounts for the season 1933/34 show a total income of £16 2/9d and a total expenditure of £16 2/9p, including a five shilling tip for the caretaker, and a total expenditure for the year's lecturers of two shillings and ninepence.

In 1939, the Erdington Photographic exhibition became the 'Premier Exhibition for the Birmingham area with over 173 entries.

On 12 February 1941, the club's president, H.C.Chamberlain announced that the club would be closed down until the 'end of hostilities', and in 1955 we have details of the club being under the chairmanship of A.E.Brookes, and holding weekly meetings at Yenton School.

In 1956, Aston and Erdington held a joint exhibition, with images from B.C.Hardy,PJ.Taplin and W.G.Ross (Bill Ross) of Aston, and A.E.Brookes, HJ.Trueman, and P.J.Taplin from the Erdington club.

The two clubs held discussions on an amalgamation, and finally came together in 1972, and have gone forward to prosper and grow into one of the most successful photographic societies in the Midlands.

D.P.Hollingworth J.P. F.I.F.P.

October 2000

Foreword

Aston has played a major part in my life. Although me and my brother, Darryl, grew up in Moseley and Springfield we spent a lot of time 'Down the Lane', along the Ladypool Road in Sparkbrook where Our Dad came from and where we had relatives and the family bookmaking business. We also spent much time in Aston, for Our Mom comes out of Whitehouse Street, which runs just off the Aston Road North. Born Sylvia Perry, she grew up in the yard at the back of the 'Albion' pub and behind the rear wall of their terrace of blind black houses was the playground of Saint Mary's Church of England School. Unsurprisingly, that was Our Mom's school – as it had been that of Our Nan, Lily Perry, nee Wood. Our Nan's mom came from Worcester and her dad was from Tewkesbury. A boatman, he was in a reserved occupation during the First World War and had been sent to Birmingham in 1915. Because Great Grandad Wood had relatives in Whitehouse Street, he and Our Great Granny settled there.

In the succeeding years, the Woods became a major family in the street. Granny and Grandad had twelve kids and when they married, most of them lived locally. In one of the front houses of Our Nan's yard lived her sister, Nancy Cotterill, with her husband and sixteen children; whilst further up the street were Uncle Bill Woods, his wife and six kids, and another sister, Mary Hodson, with her husband and one son. Granny and Grandad died just before the street was cleared, but one of my earliest memories is of going into their house with Our Mom. I recall going down a step into the one room which they had downstairs and the table in the middle of the room, and I have a vague recollection of a steep staircase in the corner.

Even after Gran and Granny died and the other Woods were moved out with everyone else, Aston featured large in our lives. Our Nan had been given a maisonette in nearby Rupert Street, Nechells and me and Our Kid often stopped with her during the school holidays. When we did, of a dinner-time (it wasn't lunch then) we would always traipse down Avenue Road to the Midland Wheel where Our Winnie worked. She was another of Our Nan's sisters and together they would take us to a coffee house where we would have bacon butties and play the 'one-legged pirate'. It took Our Mom weeks to work out that we meant the one-armed bandit. Then we'd pop along to meet another of Our Nan's brother's, Our Georgie, who worked in Eastwood's Scrapyard in Whitehouse Street. Usually, they'd take us into the little room of the 'Albion', swearing us to secrecy from Our Mom, and whilst they had a drink we'd have crisps and Vimto.

If Aston meant family it also meant one other thing in our lives: Aston Villa. Neither me nor Our Kid had a choice who we would support. With a Villa mad Mom and Nan and a Dad who was also a Villa fan, even though he was from the Blues territory of Sparkbrook, we were born to follow the Villa. The first match I can bring to mind was in 1966, when I was nine. Our Nan took us although we lost 6–2 to Chelsea we were there – Villa fans for life.

It's 35 years and more since Our Granny and Grandad Wood died and since redevelopment laid waste Whitehouse Street and destroyed the great shopping centre of Aston Cross. But still Aston means much to me. We still go down to the match and before we do, we go into the 'Albion' for a drink. We sit at the bar and Our Mom sits in Grandad Wood's chair and says hello to him and we bring the old end alive for our kids. We tell them of their Great-Great Granny Wood, of what a wonderful mother and granny she was and how she laid out the dead of the street, brought the babbies into the world and had remedies for this and that; we tell them of their Great-Great Grandad Wood who may have been small but would fight anyone; we tell them of Thompson's the pork butcher's, of the 'Havelock' with its sloping bar, of the billiard hall, of Floyd's the fish and chip shop, of the 'Astoria' Picture House and ATV, and of Thompson's the greengrocers. Above all we tell them of the Aston people, of hard-collaring and community-minded folk who'd never back down from a fight but would give you the world if they'd had it. I'm proud to have Aston in my blood.

Dr. Carl Chinn.

In May 1999 one of our members, Dave Hollingworth, suggested Aston and Erdington Photographic Society should commemorate the Millennium and after some discussion it was agreed that photographs should be taken of Aston and Erdington with a view to having a book published.

A special thanks must go to Dave Hollingworth and Schenker-BLT for the generous financial support they have given to the society to turn an idea into reality.

I would like to take this opportunity to thank everyone who has taken part in this project for their time and commitment and would also like to thank Dr. Carl Chinn for writing the foreword for our book.

As a founder member, I feel the book is a fitting memento of the distinguished past of Aston and Erdington Photographic Society.

Graham Hodgkiss
President.

Six Ways Erdington ◆ Patrick **Hickey**

Six Ways Aston ◆ Patrick **Hickey**

Aston Expressway ◆ Maurice **Dent**

H.P.Sauce Aston Cross ◆ Maurice **Dent**

Public Toilets Brookvale Park ◆ Diane **Atkins**

Brookvale Park ◆ John **Cresswell**

Witton Church ◆ Patrick **Hickey**

Witton Cemetery ◆ Mike **Cork**

Old Fort Dunlop Building ◆ Patrick **Hickey**

Dunlop Tyres ◆ Michael **Broughton**

Fort Shopping Centre ◆ Margaret **Bolland**

Gasworks Spine Road ◆ Graham **Hodgkiss**

Hotel Site Star City ◆ Graham **Hodgkiss**

Jaguar Works ◆ Graham **Hodgkiss**

Castle Vale ◆ Graham **Hodgkiss**

Tyburn House Pub ◆ John **Hartshorne**

Multiplex Cinema Erdington ◆ Michael **Broughton**

Canal Under Spaghetti Junction ◆ John **Hartshorne**

Spaghetti Junction ◆ John **Cresswell**

Cuckoo Wharf ◆ Maurice **Dent**

Barges At Cuckoo Wharf ◆ Gloria **Dent**

Wing Yip Supermarket ◆ Jane **Borland**

Albion Vaults Pub ◆ Nigel **Hamblin**

Aston Manor Brewery ◆ Graham **Hodgkiss**

Aston Manor Brewery ◆ Jane **Borland**

Britannia Pub Lichfield Road ◆ Graham **Hodgkiss**

Barton Arms Pub ◆ John **Hartshorne**

Holte End Trinity Road Aston ◆ Dinah **Hartshorne**

Aston Hotel Witton ◆ Dinah **Hartshorne**

Aston Parish Church ◆ Christine **Chick**

Lychgate Aston Parish Church ◆ Dave **Hollingworth**

Aston Hall ◆ John **Hartshorne**

Holte Pub ◆ John **Hartshorne**

Holte End Villa Park ◆ Dave **Hollingworth**

Aston Villa F.C. ◆ Dinah **Hartshorne**

Aston Library ◆ John **Hartshorne**

Bloomsbury Library ◆ Graham **Hodgkiss**

I.M.I. Factory ◆ Christine **Chick**

Aston Manor Bus Museum ◆ Dinah **Hartshorne**

Osborne Road School Erdington ◆ Gloria **Dent**

Highcroft House Erdington ◆ Dinah **Hartshorne**

Red Watch   Erdington Fire Station   ◆   Graham **Hodgkiss**

Railway Bridge Station Road Erdington ◆ Gloria **Dent**

Erdington Railway Station ◆ Graham **Hodgkiss**

Joanna's Station Road Erdington ◆ Graham **Hodgkiss**

Corner Shop Erdington ◆ Gloria **Dent**

Cantonese Restaurant High St. ◆ Patrick **Hickey**

The Villa Fish Bar Aston ◆ Patrick **Hickey**

D.I.Y. Icing Centre Edwards Road ◆ Nigel **Hamblin**

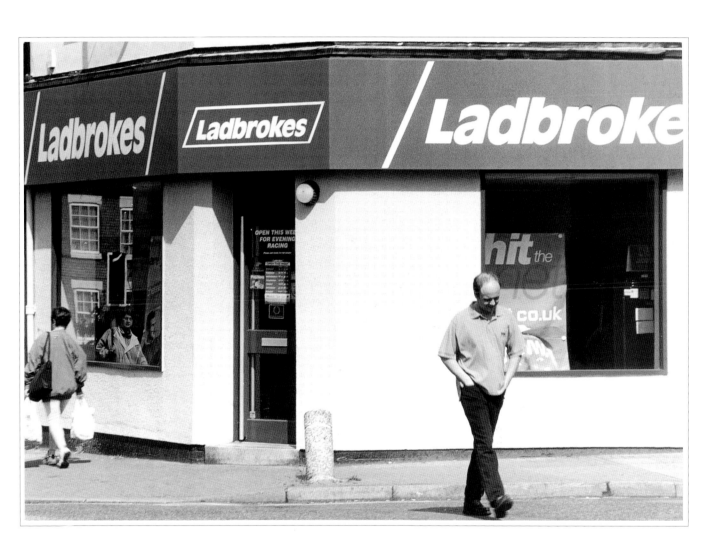

Ladbrokes Betting Office Station Road Erdington ◆ Jane **Borland**

Blockbuster Video Sutton New Road Erdington ◆ Patrick **Hickey**

Star City ◆ Michael **Broughton**

Photographers Index